D1314393

THE
GOOD News
OF
CHRISTMAS

ROUSSEAUX BRASSEUR | ART BY SIAN JAMES

HARVEST HOUSE PUBLISHERS
EUGENE, OREGON

Rousseaux Benaiah Brasseur and his beloved Hannah Rose Georgia live in the small southern Oregon community where he and his seven siblings were born and raised. Rousseaux is a pastor as well as a storyteller for the youngsters in the church. He finds his fullest joy in sharing the love of Jesus and helping others in the journey of discipleship. He also loves to spread holiday cheer and live in the spirit of Christmas all year round. His children's book *The Pilgrim's Progress: A Poetic Retelling of John Bunyan's Classic Tale* is available in hardcover and as a dramatized musical audiobook.
rousseauxbrasseur.com

Sian James' vibrant and imaginative illustrations have appeared in projects for several prominent clients, including HarperCollins and Oxford University Press. She currently resides in Cambridge, England, with her husband, Nathan, and their two affectionate cats, Miso and Mochi.

Scripture quotations are taken from The ESV® Bible (The Holy Bible, English Standard Version®), copyright © 2001 by Crossway, a publishing ministry of Good News Publishers. Used by permission. All rights reserved.

Cover design by Faceout Studio, Interior design by Left Coast Design

M This logo is a federally registered trademark of the Hawkins Children's LLC. Harvest House Publishers, Inc., is the exclusive licensee of this trademark.

The Good News of Christmas

Text copyright © 2022 by Rousseaux Brasseur
Artwork © 2022 by Sian James

Published by Harvest House Publishers
Eugene, Oregon 97408
www.harvesthousepublishers.com

ISBN 978-0-7369-8609-0 (hardcover)

Library of Congress Control Number: 2022931409

All rights reserved. No part of this publication may be reproduced, stored in a retrieval system, or transmitted in any form or by any means—electronic, mechanical, digital, photocopy, recording, or any other—except for brief quotations in printed reviews, without the prior permission of the publisher.

Printed in China
23 24 25 26 27 28 29 30 / RDS / 10 9 8 7 6 5 4 3 2

To my overwhelmed, overworked, under-appreciated mother,

Who made each Christmas unforgettable in one way or another.

For embracing and enduring the chaos of seven kids,

For the innumerable thank-yous which we daily failed to give,

For never canceling Christmas (though you threatened to do so each year)

And for the copper angel earrings in your green and swollen ears.

In the midst of each chaotic Christmas, may this book bring a pause of peace
to your soul. Take rest and rejoice in Jesus, God's gift too wonderful for words.

Your beloved boy,

Soey

I wish to tell my readers now, before this tale begins,
That unlike every other book, this story has no end.
If truth be told, this book you hold is just the
    middle chapter
In God's plan, which spans from before time began
    to the infinite ever after.

It's the story of God's glory at the heart of human history
In which God revealed who **He** is and uncovered the mystery.
So as you hear it, may God's Spirit stir inside your heart
And bring *you* into His kingdom too...now it's time for our
story to start.

In ancient days a promise came to Israel of old,
Whose prophets wrote of a coming hope and of a King foretold.
From Abraham's line this King would rise to bless the broken nations,
And great King David's greater Son would rule all of creation.

They prophesied this Prince of Peace would free their captive land,
Fulfilling all God's purposes, His promises, and plans.
They waited for their saving Lord, whom they put all their hope in...
...but several long centuries had passed since last their God had spoken.

But God, who often seems to us to move so awfully slow,
Had planned to send Messiah soon—but little did they know
That He, their long-awaited King who was about to come,
Was actually God's one and only blessed, beloved Son.

Now it came to pass at last that after many generations,
Young Mary sat lost in her thoughts of wedding celebrations.
The graceful maiden daydreamed of the most delightful plans,
For Joseph, her betrothed, was known to be a righteous man.

But as her glad mind wandered, the angel Gabriel appeared!
"Greetings, O favored one!" he said—but Mary shook in fear.
"Fear not, for God will come to you, and in this very year,
You shall conceive a Son who will bring heaven's kingdom here!"

"How can this be," replied Mary, "for a virgin such as I?"
"The Holy Spirit will come on you, in the power of
 the Most High.
Your Son will be the holy Son of God, and He shall reign
On David's throne forevermore! Jesus shall be His name."

"Behold," responded Mary, "I am the servant of the Lord.
Let everything be done to me according to Your word."
Then as the angel left her home, her world was rearranged,
And prayerfully she pondered how her whole life would be changed.

As time went on, it wasn't long till Mary's child grew,
Thus Joseph contemplated what the best thing was to do.
He thought to call the wedding off and separate from Mary,
For he knew the Child was not his own which his fiancée carried.

And how could he have known that none of this was as it seemed?

...Until the night an angel spoke to Joseph as he dreamed.

"Joseph, son of David, do not fear to make Mary your wife.

The Holy Spirit has filled her womb with God's miraculous life.

"She shall bring forth a Son, and the name Jesus you shall give Him,
For He will save His people, and their sins will be forgiven."
When Joseph woke, he went to work with no more hesitation
And spent the day without delay in prayerful preparation.

All this fulfilled the prophecy that long ago proclaimed,
"The virgin shall conceive a Son, Immanuel by name."
(Immanuel means God with us—for that's who Jesus is,
The Son of God and Son of Man who saves us from our sins.)

Now at that time Caesar Augustus, the emperor of Rome,
Decreed that each man must return to his ancestral home.
So Joseph's pregnant bride-to-be left Nazareth with him,
And after nearly a hundred miles they came to Bethlehem.

When they arrived they found there was no lodging at the inn,
So Joseph searched around the town for a resting place for them.
He finally found a stable where the animals were kept,
And, about to faint, without complaint, they laid down there and slept.

But in the night Mary awoke! The time had finally come—
And she gave birth to Jesus, her beloved firstborn Son.

They wrapped Him snug in strips of cloth and for this King's first bed,
They laid Him in a manger, where the animals had fed.

That night in nearby fields where the shepherds kept their sheep,
An angel in bright glory came and roused them from their sleep.

"Do not be fearful, I have come with good news of great joy!
For unto you this day is born the promised baby Boy.
This news is for all people; let the word be spread abroad:
He is the Christ, the hoped-for King! The Savior sent from God!"

Then suddenly, as though the stars all blazed forth in full brightness,
More angels appeared, and all cheered, "Glory to God in the highest!

And on the earth, peace be to those with whom our God is pleased!"
Then they vanished as the awestruck shepherds rose from trembling knees.

"Let's go to Bethlehem," they cried, "to find this newborn King!"
And when they found Joseph and Mary, they told them everything.

Now after Jesus had been born, there came wise men from afar
Who from the distant East, by faith, had followed a bright star.
They came to cruel King Herod first, inquiring of the news,
"Where has God's promised child been born, the great King of the Jews?"

"We saw His star and from afar have come to worship Him!"
But Herod's hard and hateful heart hid wicked plans within.
He summoned Israel's priests and scribes to test and
question them,
And from their scrolls they told him Christ would come
from Bethlehem.

Then to the wise men Herod lied, faking a friendly smile,
"I wish to worship Him as well. Go find this royal Child!"
So they left and let the starlight lead, till there in David's town
They found the Boy, and filled with joy, they worshipfully bowed down!

Then holding out their treasure chests they said, "Three gifts we bring."
The gift of gold was given first to honor Christ as King.

Next frankincense, a fitting gift for the heaven-sent High Priest;
Last, myrrh, which marked the sacrifice He would make for
mankind's peace.

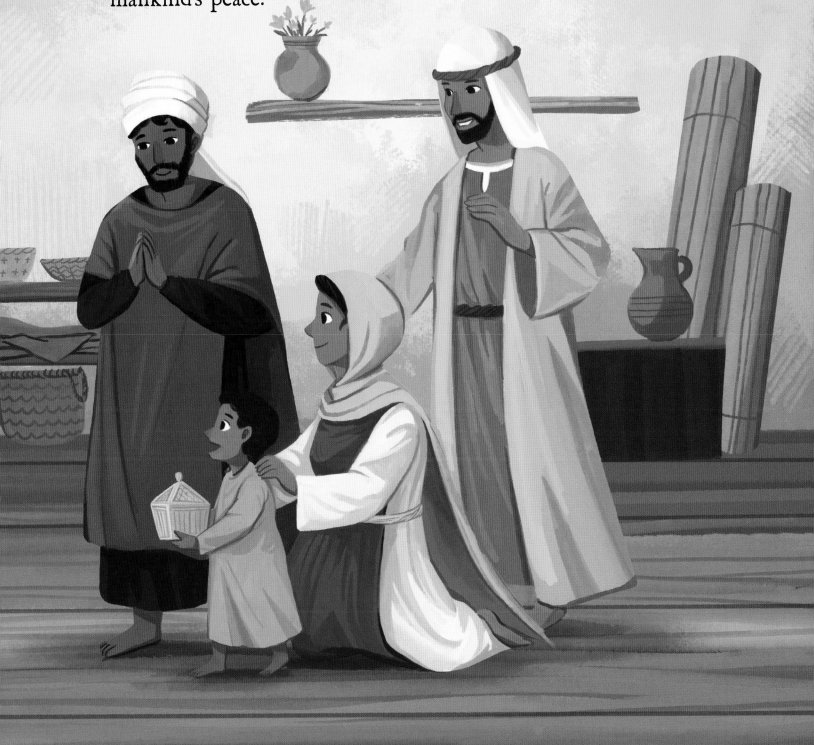

Now when the wise men went to leave, God warned them in a dream
To head home by a different route, which ruined Herod's scheme.
For evil plots could never stop God's great plan of salvation,
To build His kingdom here on earth and restore His whole creation.

Now, friends, this is no fairy tale, or folklore myth of glory—
Although miraculous, this is the *one true* Christmas story.
From heaven the King came down to us in human form
      and flesh
To save the world, which He had made, from Satan, sin, and death!

And from ancient days up till today, to all who trust in Christ,
The Father gives forgiveness of sins and everlasting life.
So open up your heart to Him—believe the good news is true.
Receive this glorious Christmas gift that God holds out to you.

And the angel said to them,

"Fear not, for behold, I bring
you good news of great joy that
will be for all the people."

LUKE 2:10